Author:

David Stewart has written many nonfiction books for children. He lives in Brighton, England, with his family.

Artist:

David Antram was born in Brighton, England, in 1958. He studied at Eastbourne College of Art and then worked in advertising for 15 years before becoming a full-time artist. He has illustrated many children's nonfiction books.

Series creator:

David Salariya was born in Dundee, Scotland. He has illustrated a wide range of books and has created and designed many new series for publishers in the UK and overseas. David established The Salariya Book Company in 1989. He lives in Brighton with his wife, illustrator Shirley Willis, and their son, Jonathan.

Editor: **Nick Pierce**

Photo credits:
p.22–23 Sobolevskyi_Vadym/Shutterstock, Julian Popov/Shutterstock, Samir Behlic/Shutterstock, Volodymyr Burdiak/Shutterstock, hedgehog94/Shutterstock
p.24–25 Norjipin Saidi/Shutterstock, tasnenad/Shutterstock, Jacek Boron/Shutterstock, Witsawat.S/Shutterstock, Tomasz Klejdysz/Shutterstock, Henrik Larsson/Shutterstock, TB studio/Shutterstock

Published in Great Britain in 2021 by
The Salariya Book Company Ltd
25 Marlborough Place, Brighton BN1 1UB

ISBN 978-0-531-13176-3 (lib. bdg.) 978-0-531-13189-3 (pbk.)

Published in 2021 in the United States by Franklin Watts®
An imprint of Scholastic Inc.

A CIP catalog record for this book is available from the Library of Congress.

Printed in the U.S.A. 113
1 2 3 4 5 6 7 8 9 10 R 28 27 26 25 24 23 22 21

SCHOLASTIC, FRANKLIN WATTS, and associated logos are trademarks and/or registered trademarks of Scholastic Inc

Scholastic Inc., 557 Broadway, New York, NY 10012

How Would You Survive as a Bee?

Written by
David Stewart

Illustrated by
David Antram

Series created by
David Salariya

Franklin Watts®
An Imprint of Scholastic Inc.

Contents

You Are a Bee

There are over 20,000 species of bees, all of which evolved from wasps many millions of years ago. You are a member of one of the most social species: a honeybee. You live in a colony with other bees like yourself, and you harvest pollen and nectar from flowers in order to make your food. The life of a bee can be difficult: It's a lot of work taking care of your nest and raising new bees, and there are many dangers. It's time to answer the big question: How would you survive as a bee?

A Bee's Body

Simple eyes

You have three simple eyes for detecting light.

Compound eyes

You have two large compound eyes, made up of thousands of eye cells, used for detecting movement and patterns.

Mouthparts

You have jaws (mandibles) and a sheath (maxilla) for your tubelike tongue (glossa). When you land on a flower, your glossa extends from the maxilla to suck up the nectar.

Mandibles

Maxilla

Glossa

Size

You are roughly the same size as a typical honeybee: about half an inch (15 millimeters) long.

Hair

Your body is covered in hair that you use to gather pollen and regulate your body temperature.

Exoskeleton

A hard covering, called an exoskeleton, protects your entire body.

Wings

You have two pairs of wings. They are made of very thin pieces of exoskeleton. A row of hooks, called hamuli, connect front and rear wings so they beat together when you are flying.

Stinger

As a female bee, you have a stinger at the rear of your abdomen. This consists of a venom sac and a pair of pointed barbs that deliver the venom to your victim.

7

The young worker bees build and repair the nest: a beeswax comb of hexagonal cells for storing honey, pollen, and larvae. They clean the nest, feed the larvae care for the queen, remove waste, handle incoming nectar, and guard the entrance.

Life in a Colony

You live in a wild honeybee colony. The nest is a very busy place, with different bees performing specific tasks. It contains a colony of around 20,000 to 30,000 bees. These are female worker bees (like you), male drones, and a queen. The workers do all the work in the nest. The drones, however, have just one function: to mate with the queen. They do no work in the nest and are usually only there during the months of late spring and summer.

If You...

are an older worker bee, you will be sent out of the nest to collect nectar, pollen, and water for the colony.

▼ During the autumn and winter months, you and the other female worker bees gather around the queen to keep her warm, forcing out the male drones who no longer serve a purpose.

▲ During the spring and summer months, you and the other older female worker bees spend most of your time outside the nest. This is when the colony is most active.

▶ For your colony to function effectively, you all need to be able to communicate with each other. You do this through dances and by producing pheromones.

By laying eggs, the queen bee ensures the survival of the colony.

Bee Babies

Bees reproduce by laying eggs. All of the eggs in a nest are laid by the same bee: the queen. She can lay up to 2,500 eggs a day in the summer months, and more than a million eggs in her whole lifetime. As a worker bee, one of your most important jobs is to look after the eggs as they hatch into larvae and grow into new bees that will eventually replace you in the colony.

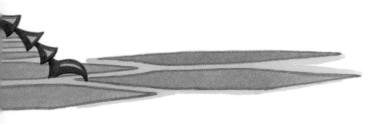

If You...

live in a nest that gets foulbrood, you're in trouble! This bacterial disease kills the larvae and causes decay within the walls of the comb.

You feed new larvae with a special substance called royal jelly for three days. Then they are given a mixture of nectar and pollen called beebread.

When you want to nurture a future queen bee, you have to make it a larger cell to live in. The larva of the future queen is given more royal jelly to eat.

When the larvae are big enough, you cap their cells with wax, and the larvae pupate. When each pupa is ready to emerge, it chews through the wax lid and then joins the colony.

Collecting Nectar

As an older worker bee, it is also your job to visit flowering plants outside the nest to collect nectar and pollen. You also manage to pollinate (fertilize) the plants at the same time. While you are collecting the nectar and pollen with your legs, some pollen from the stamens (male part of the flower) sticks to the hairs of your body, too. When you visit the next flower, some of this pollen is rubbed off onto the stigma (female part of the flower). This fertilizes the plant and causes it to produce seeds and fruit. This means that you're not only helping your colony to survive, but lots of species of plants as well!

If You...

are struggling to carry all that pollen, use your forelegs to brush pollen from your body onto your back legs, then compress it in "pollen baskets" to carry back to the nest.

▲ Unlike humans, you can see ultraviolet light. Some flowers have patterns visible in ultraviolet light that guide you to the nectar inside them.

▼ Your tongue is covered with bristles that extend outward to catch the nectar from flowers.

You are attracted to a flower by its color, shape, and scent. Since you can't see the color red, you are most attracted to yellow, blue, purple, and white flowers.

You keep track of the Sun'
movement through the sky,
so you don't get lost!

How Do Bees Find Their Way?

I f you want to survive, it's important not to get lost when you leave the nest. Luckily, your internal clock tells you how far you have flown and how far the Sun has moved during your journey, so that you can always find your way home. Scientists have discovered that the neurons in bees' brains transmit information relating to changes in direction and distance covered, allowing bees to navigate effectively. These are in the part of the brain called the central complex—the same part that controls navigation in the brains of humans and other animals.

▶ You have 170 odor receptors, allowing you to smell the difference between hundreds of different types of flowers. This is very helpful for finding your way when you're out collecting nectar and pollen.

▶ If you find somewhere with lots of nectar, you need to let your fellow worker bees know. Return to the nest and do a dance. Your movements will tell them the direction to fly in relation to the Sun, and the distance.

15

Filling honeycomb cells with honey to keep a food supply going is a time-consuming job for the bees in your nest.

16

Why Do Bees Need Honey to Survive?

Collecting nectar is vital for your survival as a colony. This sweet substance is used as food for the colony during the winter months. The type of nectar you gather will affect the color and flavor of the honey. You store the nectar from flowers in your honey stomach, which is next to your normal stomach. Nectar is about 70 percent water. To turn it into honey, the water content must be reduced to about 20 percent.

If You...

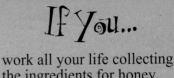

work all your life collecting the ingredients for honey, it will still take another seven bees to produce just one teaspoon of honey!

◀ You take the nectar you've collected back to the nest and regurgitate it into another bee's mouth. The bees in the nest turn the nectar into honey by chewing, swallowing, and regurgitating it over and over. *Yum!*

▼ Once the honey is stored in the honeycombs, it is still very wet. You and other workers work hard fanning your wings over the cells to evaporate more water from it.

▲ When the honey is ready, the bees seal the filled cells with a wax lid to keep them clean. The finished honey is thick, sticky, and very sweet.

Joining the Swarm

Is the place starting to feel a little crowded? If the colony you belong to gets too big, this means that the queen's pheromone signals can no longer reach all of the workers. For the bees who don't receive the signals, it's as if the queen doesn't exist, so they start raising new queen larvae. Before the new queens hatch, the old queen departs the nest with her loyal followers, including you, gathered tightly around her. This is called a swarm. You will journey with your queen to find a new home for your colony elsewhere.

If You...

are a newly hatched queen bee, you might have to fight to the death with the other newly hatched queens to decide who will become queen of the colony.

▸ The queen is a weak flyer, so the swarm will have to rest at some point, on a tree branch or fence. Scouts are then sent out to search for a suitable place for a nest.

▸ As a scout, you have found a new nest site. You do a waggle dance to tell the other bees about it. The more excited your dance, the more you like it.

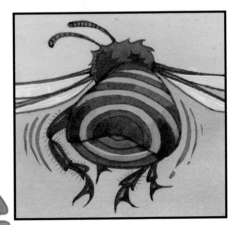

▲ Beekeepers can train bees to swarm around their faces to create bee beards by putting a queen bee in a cage around their neck.

Look Out! Danger Everywhere!

Although you have strength in numbers, both your nest and its individual bees are at risk from predators and parasites that prey on your species. When you visit a flower, you'll have to be on the lookout for ambush predators like beewolves, crab spiders, and praying mantises, which specialize in catching unsuspecting bees. Mammal predators, like bears and skunks, also eat bees.

▶ Watch out for the birds that eat bees, attack their nests, and eat the larvae. These include shrikes, flycatchers, bee-eaters, swifts, swallows, and honey buzzards.

▼ Defend your colony from a predatory hornet by surrounding the hornet in a tight "bee ball" of up to 500 bees. The ball raises the temperature inside, which slowly cooks the hornet.

▶ If varroa mites attach themselves to your body, they can feed on your fat body (a bit like the liver) until you die.

If You...

are a honeybee and you sting someone or something, you will die! Your stinger has barbs on it, and when you fly away after stinging, the barbs get stuck and rip away part of your abdomen. Ouch!

20

The beewolf, also known as the bee-killer wasp, is a large species of predatory wasp. The female hunts honeybee workers, paralyzing them with her stinger and taking them back to her burrow to feed to her larvae.

Beewolf

21

The Story of Beekeeping

People have collected honey from wild nests for at least ten thousand years. Gradually, people figured out how to keep bees in artificial hives. They learned more about the behavior of bees and how to exploit this to increase honey yields. But bees have also become threatened by the activities of humans. Here, we'll take a look at manmade hives and why bees are in trouble.

1. *Modern hives are made with removable frames to hold honey and for bees to raise their brood. The most common is the Langstroth hive, developed in the 1850s by Lorenzo Langstroth, a minister who became a beekeeper.*

2. Manmade beehives have the following: A roof, to provide shelter for the bees; a honey super, where the honey produced by the bees is stored; a queen excluder, which is a mesh barrier that the queen can't fit through, to stop her from laying eggs in honey cells; a brood box, where the bees lay their eggs; and a stand, to keep the hive off the ground.

3. Since ancient times, beekeepers have used smoke to calm the bees while they take the honey. Smoke masks the bees' pheromones, making them less aggressive.

4. In 2006, beekeepers noticed a new and disturbing trend. In honeybee colonies in North America and Europe, worker bees were disappearing, leaving behind the queen and a few nurse bees. Without nectar-gatherers, the colonies soon died. This became known as Colony Collapse Disorder (CCD).

5. Scientists think that CCD is probably caused by a combination of parasites, the spreading of pesticides, and a poor diet. People can help bees by planting bee-friendly flowers, vegetables, and herbs, such as lilac, lavender, wisteria, squash, pumpkins, sunflowers, and honeysuckle.

23

Bee Family Tree

Bees are part of a large order of insects called the Hymenoptera. Species that belong to the Hymenoptera tend to have two pairs of wings (a large fore pair and a smaller hind pair), antennae, and mouthparts for biting. If you were a honeybee, these species would be some of your closest living cousins...

Yellow Jacket

These wasps live in colonies and usually have the familiar and distinctive black and yellow markings. All female yellow jackets have stingers.

Patchwork Leaf-cutter Bee

Unlike the honeybee, this species is solitary. It cuts out sections of leaves and uses them to construct its nest, where it lays its eggs.

Sand-digging Wasp

The wasp species Ammophila pubescens *catches a caterpillar and lays an egg upon it. As the larva grows and eats the caterpillar, the wasp continues to bring more prey to its nest.*

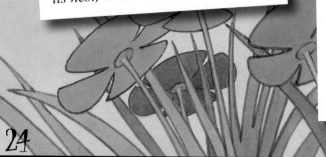

Ant

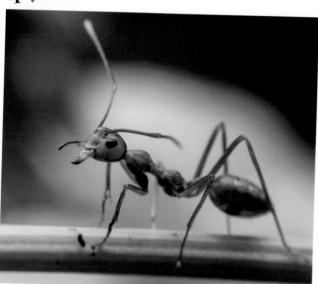

Species of ant have colonized almost every landmass on Earth. They live in colonies that can exhibit very complex behaviors, including the division of labor and communication between individual ants—similar to bee colonies.

Sawfly

Sawflies mainly eat plants. Some species mimic the look of bees and wasps, disguising their ovipositor (tube-like organ for laying eggs) as a stinger in order to put off predators.

Spider-hunting Wasp

This species paralyzes its spider prey and buries them alive with its larvae. Some types even amputate the spider's legs before taking it to the nest!

Honeybee (You)

Honeybees are native to Eurasia (the continents of Europe and Asia), but they have been spread by humans around the world because of their honey-making abilities.

25

Bee Quiz

1 How many species of bees are there?

2 What is the name of the hard covering that protects a bee's body?

3 What is the function of the drones in a colony?

4 What is the name of the special substance fed to new larvae?

5 What kind of light can bees see that humans cannot?

6 How many odor receptors do bees have?

7 What do bees use honey for?

8 What species of predatory wasp hunts honeybee workers?

9 What happens if a honeybee stings something?

10 What do beekeepers use to calm bees while they take their honey?

Bee Quiz Answers

1 Over 20,000
(page 5)

2 Exoskeleton
(page 7)

3 To mate with the queen
(page 9)

4 Royal jelly
(page 11)

5 Ultraviolet
(page 12)

6 170
(page 15)

7 Food
(page 17)

8 Beewolf
(page 21)

9 The honeybee dies
(page 20)

10 Smoke
(page 23)

Bee Facts

A colony of bees will fly 25,000 miles (40,000 kilometers) and visit a million flowers to produce 2 pounds (1 kilogram) of honey.

Honeybees beat their wings 230 times a second, creating that familiar buzzing sound. They fly at an average of 15 miles (24 kilometers) an hour.

Honeybees can perceive the difference between images in one 300th of a second, compared to just a 50th of a second for humans. So if a honeybee watched television, it would see each individual frame.

Wild and domesticated bees carry out about 80 percent of all pollination worldwide.

According to US National Agricultural Statistics, there has been a 60 percent reduction in honeybees in the United States, from 6 million colonies in 1947 to 2.4 million colonies in 2008. Biologists believe that deadly pesticides commonly used by farmers around the world are responsible for the severe decline in bee numbers in North America and elsewhere.

Types Of Bee Dances

When a bee locates a new food source, it returns to the nest and hands out samples of the flower's nectar to other members of the colony. Then it performs a dance that indicates the distance, direction, quality, and quantity of the food supply. There are two kinds of dances: the round dance and the waggle dance.

Round Dance:

With the "round dance," the bee turns in circles to the left and right. This is performed if the food source is less than 105 feet (32 meters) away. The better the food source, the longer and more excited the dance. The round dance doesn't tell the bees what direction to fly in, but the bees will recognize the smell from their nectar samples, so they will know how to find the flowers.

Waggle Dance:

With the "waggle dance," the bee does two loops with a straight run in the middle. This is performed if the food source is more than 105 feet (32 meters) away. The rate of looping indicates the distance to the food source. The faster the rate, the closer the food supply. The bee also buzzes as it loops, and this is another indicator of distance: The longer it buzzes, the further away the food is.

The direction of the straight run demonstrates the direction the bees should fly in, relative to the Sun. If the food is in the same direction as the Sun, the bee dances straight up. If it lies in the opposite direction of the Sun, the bee dances straight down. If it's to the right, the bee dances at the appropriate angle to the right, and so on.

Glossary

Abdomen The hindmost section of an insect's body, containing most of its organs.

Bacterial Caused by bacteria: single-celled microorganisms, some of which can cause disease.

Colony A community of animals, such as bees, living close together and forming an organized unit.

Drone In a colony of social bees, a male bee that does no work but can fertilize a queen.

Hexagonal Describing a hexagon, a shape that has six straight sides of equal length.

Honeycomb A structure of hexagonal cells of wax, made by bees to store honey and eggs.

Larva (plural: larvae) The young form of an insect, often wingless and wormlike, and very different from its parents at birth. The larval stage is the stage between egg and pupa.

Mandibles Either half of the crushing organ in the mouthparts of an insect.

Nectar A sugary fluid secreted within flowers to encourage pollination by insects and collected by bees in order to make honey.

Parasite An organism that lives in or on another organism (its host) and benefits by obtaining nutrients at the host's expense.

Pesticide A substance used to destroy insects and other organisms harmful to cultivated plants.

Pheromone A chemical released by an animal affecting the behavior of others of its species.

Pollination The transferral of pollen from flower to flower by wind, insects, or other animals to allow fertilization.

Ultraviolet A form of radiation that has a wavelength shorter than that of visible light, so that it cannot be seen by humans.

Index